love me like the stars

POEMS & STORIES

love me like the stars

POEMS & STORIES

alesia carter

the grl publishing / los angeles, california

www.alesiacarter.com

ISBN: 978-0-692-11581-7

for my boys
trey and jaden
may you continually chase your dreams
and attain what you seek

these are my thoughts
that weigh heavily
on my heart
i think of them as a river
that i could no longer contain
overflowing
spilling over
seeping onto these pages
this is lust
this is love
this is romance
and the heartache that comes with it
this is the journey to salvation
no matter how daunting
and terrifying it may be
this is my vulnerability
wrapped in humility

handle with care.

contents of this journey

last

can i stand in the sun with you?
can you teach me
all of the ways in which
i can hopelessly love you?

— apollo

we are one ☆
with the stars ☆

THE BOY

Love Me Li...

Saturday, December 23, 2017

the boy ...

INTERSTELLAR

i was captivated by the magical allure in
your eyes. all i could think about was how
much we could have a love that transcends
through space and time.

love me like the stars

your eyes
those magical
mesmerizing eyes
they tell me
everything i need to know
and i fall for you
over again
each and every time

lust.

you are my galaxy
my jupiter
my moon
my stars
my all
my everything
you are my favorite dreams

supernova.

love me like the stars

if only
i could
show you
how much
i adore you
and
how much
i would
absolutely
love you

if you were mine.

tell me you remember it
the endless conversation
a beautiful symphony
our love language

tell me you felt it
a profound feeling
that was magnetic
almost nostalgic
as if our souls have done this before
two strangers who crossed paths
found to be reunited again

i wanted it to last
we didn't have to touch
as we somehow
made love with our words
you could be you
i could be me
maybe all along
this was our destiny

prophecy.

i love too much
i feel too much
i fall
so deeply
so purely
so strongly
be still my heart
fear not
do not ache for love unknown
your time will come
and it will be for you to keep
just hold on

lust for love.

you told me
it's you
as you held my hand
but then
i awoke
to realize
it was just a dream
still
i hope
eventually
it'll be
my
reality

speak your love into existence.

love me like the stars

let's runaway
and fall in love
let's find something
worth fighting for

getaway car.

do you ever think of me
do you ever wonder
what it would feel like
to hold my hand
do you think about loving me
how we could make
such sweet melodies
getting lost in ecstasy
are you curious
to experience
my warmth
my bliss
my kiss

forbidden fruit.

love me like the stars

what's it like to love
and be loved
unapologetically
with every fiber of your being
a mutual coexistence
without hesitance
an uncomplicated kind of love
without the pain and sorrow
only with joy

what's it like to know
to be safe enough
to bear your soul
to be normal
to share a life
to depend
to have happiness
to simply
feel alive again

a foreign feeling.

fill your world
with magic
enchantment
and dreams
feel
really feel
create
read books
make your world
wonderful
make beautiful art
and don't forget
to love

lust for life.

love me like the stars

you're just a stranger to me
but oddly
i miss you
my heart beats
its own song for you
i yearn for you
and your hands
i yearn to be able to look up
and see your precious eyes
gazing emphatically
into mine

poetic daydreamer.

she stood on the corner patiently waiting
to what may have seemed like an eternity
she heard his voice in the darkness
calling out her name
that damn beautiful accent
could've made her melt right then and there

she turned around
he was just as she imagined
piercing eyes that punctured her soul
and a warm embrace
that made her feel at home

he had a charming smile
that made her shy in his presence
she embraced the minutes
that turned into hours
hoping it wouldn't end
hoping for a little while longer

to be in that moment
was such a whirlwind
her heart went pitter patter
when he made her laugh
a feeling she wanted so desperately to last

if only he would stay
if only he would stay
if only he would stay

j.l.: 8/10/16.

love me like the stars

tonight
i'm wishing on a star
hoping
to be where you are

i know it sounds cliché
but
this is what you do to me

why can't i get you out of my head.

oh what it must feel like
when she gets to touch you
what it must feel like
to be engulfed in your arms so tight
that your heavenly scent
is all she can breathe in and breathe out
in order to survive

tell me
what is it like to love you
does it make her feel
like she's on cloud nine
does loving you
make her feel high
almost as if she could touch the sky
does loving you
give her life
does loving you
make her weak in the knees
does loving you
make her heart skip a beat
so much so
that she can't even speak

oh what it must feel like
to be adored by you
to have you
to lie next to you
to wake up next to you
i bet loving you is like magic
i can only imagine
that loving you is an honor
that i shamelessly hoped
to have the privilege
but i'll bite my tongue
smoke this cigarette

inhale
exhale

love me like the stars

try to put thoughts of you
loving me
out of my head
try to put thoughts of you
touching me
out of my mind
thoughts i've had
that make me feel like
i've committed a crime

what is it like to love you.

let me paint this lust
into a work of art

the paint and the canvas.

love me like the stars

that's where i want to live
that's where i want to breathe
that's where i want to love
that's where i want to bloom

where is that he asks

in your heart
tell me you see it too

safe space.

it was magical
when our eyes met
had the stars finally aligned
is it a sign
do i wait
quietly fantasize
to pass the time
to avoid the realization that
i am not yours
and
you are not mine

selfless
gentle
kind
imagining your fingertips
dancing on my hips
i succumb to how it might feel
to taste your lips

in my dreams
it's you and me
of what we could be
indulge me
keep me
kiss me
love me
i could love you
infinitely

the boy part 1: new moon.

love me like the stars

you
your heart
these thoughts
your touch
i can't resist
all i can do
is want

crave.

i know it's wrong
but you
you feel
so
damn
right

look what you did.

i look at you
and i see you so clearly
a heart of gold in a world
that has given up on love
still somehow
you embody what it means
to be a pure human being
with such grace and beauty
it's selfish of me
but
i contemplate
how i can get you
to love me
maybe
you will fall in love
with my words
and see the desire that burns
when i write about the magic
you unknowingly and undoubtedly
make me yearn

the boy part 2: venus.

she came out of nowhere
and suddenly
she was the one
that he had been waiting for

awakening.

love me like the stars

if
i
could
just
feel
your
touch
i can't explain why
i feel so strong
for a man
that knows i exist
but doesn't realize
that i am already
his

desire.

will you love me
the way i yearn to be loved
will you be the light to my sun
will you follow me wherever i go
will you be the reason that i knew love

stardust.

love me like the stars

you intoxicate me
i'm addicted
you're in my veins
give me more
of you
i have no shame
you are the sea
that engulfs me
with wonder
and nostalgia
you are my every desire
the light
to my flickering fire

drunk in lust.

in another world you're mine
i can't describe
how
this feels right
is it ok
for me to feel this way
are you ok
knowing
that when i close my eyes
it's you that i dream of at night

can i adore you
can i write you love letters
can i profess all of these feelings
and the warmth that i feel inside
whenever you cross my mind

it's like you brought me sunshine
in the palm of your hands
because of you
i believe again
you turned my whole world upside down
i'll never be the same
even if
you don't know exactly
what you do to me

magician.

love me like the stars

there is something poetic about you
i don't know if it's your charming smile
or the way you simply move
there is something addicting
about the way you make me laugh
the way your heart cares
your compassion for humanity
your passion for the simple things
maybe it's the way
you exemplify what loving deeply truly means

the halo you wear
shines as bright as a thousand stars in the night
it measures beyond what i can imagine
the reflection glistens through my eyes
and to think
out of all the galaxies
how beautiful it is
that we exist in the same moment of time
it's as though
the heavens knew
when they created you
that you would be the light in my starlit sky

you are electric
you are the warmth of the sun
a prepossessing flower that blooms
with an unwavering love
i'm drawn to your spirit
silently wishing
your hand was forever mine
to cherish

the boy part 3: milky way.

you and i
we combust
to make stardust
and together
we light up the sky
as we fly
through the darkest of nights
we touch the moon
we are one with the stars
soaring through a galaxy
made up entirely
of our luminescent love

fireflies.

love me like the stars

last night
i saw you again
and the moment
was just as perfect
as the last time you were in my presence
i was captivated by
the magical allure in your eyes
all i could think about
was how much
we could have a love that transcends
through space and time
i hope that there is no end to our story
that i can remain in your existence
to glow in your glory

you inspire the most beautiful sonnets
that i could write
page after page the words come to life
you are a mirage of enchantment
that once seemed impossible
only to find
you were the missing piece of the puzzle
our connection ignites a song in my heart
that entices me to dance on the stars
effortlessly floating between saturn and mars

you are extraordinary
almost impalpable
all the while
you do not know
you are utterly beyond
anything that i could ever dream of
but there is a quiet ache in my soul
because my love for you
i will never be able to show

the boy part 4: interstellar.

romance

december 23, 2017

my dearest ~~████~~

i have thought of you each day. and i can't
help but think...
can i watch the sunrise with you?
can we hold onto this moment in our grasp?
can i be the first thing you see every morning?
can you hold me just a little while longer.
can i be all that you desire?
can i be your sunflower?
can we have forever and always?
me by your side ███ you by mine
can i be your reason for breathing?
can i be your reason for living.
can we curl up next to the fire
and read books to one another?
can we listen to the beat of our hearts
and act out our love for each other?
can we be passionate with our existence
making love at all hours?
can i watch the sunset with you
and do the same thing all over again tomorrow?

eternally yours,
a

can i watch the sunrise with you
can we hold onto this moment in our grasp
can i be the first thing you see every morning
can you hold me just a little while longer
can i be all that you desire
can i be your sunflower
can we have forever and always
me by your side
you by mine
can i be your reason for breathing
can i be your reason for living
can we curl up next to the fire
and read books to one another
can we listen to the beat of our hearts
and act out our love for each other
can we be passionate with our existence
making love at all hours
can i watch the sunset with you
and do the same thing all over again tomorrow

romance.

after what felt like an eternity
you finally found me

where have you been.

when your lips kissed mine
it was divine
when i felt your grasp
my heart cried *at last*

soulmate.

you inspire me endlessly

muse.

love me like the stars

you make me feel
as though
i can kiss the sky
your fingertips
graze across my skin
and suddenly
there is no gravity
i am in
heaven

i exist for you.

i'm in too deep
i'm
hopelessly
absolutely
falling
for you

the welcoming.

love me like the stars

we sat inside
hiding from the chilly weather
a light twinkled in his eyes
i was mesmerized
i couldn't hold back
i had to profess
i could no longer keep my love a secret

*what do you think of me
do you think i'm enough to love
i just need to know
am i beautiful
beautiful enough inside and out
for you to love me without doubt
i know i'm not the typical girl
i'm from a different world
caught up in these encapsulated words*

why do you ask he questioned

without hesitancy
all my heart could do is sing

*because i love you in spite of
even if the world will be against us
it makes me want to love you more
perfectly imperfect is what you are
so i just need to know
if you could love someone like me
if you can see past my insecurities
and into the depths of my soul
that i promise you
another man shall never know*

he smiled a smile that made me melt
and warmed my hands in his
as he undoubtedly said

you are beautiful just the way you are
i have always loved you
i love you like the stars

a midwinter night's dream.

love me like the stars

i will love his dreams
and he will love mine

significant other.

take my hand in yours
can you feel
the warmth
between our fingers
the way they dance
can you feel
the romance

it's electrifying
isn't it

paradise.

i have been thinking
about how i want to love
about who i would want to love
and it's so simple

the answer is you
i would love you
with every fiber of my being
give you my last
because you are my first

i want to love you
because you bring out the best in me
you truly see me
i don't think you realize
what that does to me

and so
for what it's worth
the answer
always
leads back
to you

something special.

flowers and mornings
with you
i just need you

comfort.

i never thought
this passion
this feeling
could be
but then
you happened
to me

hopeless romantic.

i'm so comfortable in your presence
that i utter words
i've never said out loud
because your existence
calms my qualms
i don't know what the future holds
but i hope
every waking moment is with you my love

your voice is as beautiful as violin strings
more beautiful
than the sound of piano keys
that make my soul sing

take all of me
forever
always
unconditionally

my favorite instrumental song.

love me like the stars

i painted a sunset that looked like you
pinks
purples
with hints of
reds
greens
blues
until it became an aurora
that perfectly embodies all that you are
and all that i am

sunset pink tones forever with you.

he is
the other half of my heart
the stars in my sky
lighting my way
to breathe new life
love me
love me
love me
and i will love you
endlessly

king.

love me like the stars

you taught me how to love
and it made me better than i ever was

your power over me.

he is my only wish
for me
to be
his

shooting star.

love me like the stars

if i have the capacity to love
it is because you guided me
beyond the boundaries
where i could see that i was in need
of someone
that was capable of giving
someone that knew
the meaning
of reciprocity
without me having to sacrifice
my happy

love story.

alesia carter

in your embrace
is where i belong
in your arms
is where i call home

i am yours.

love me like the stars

i found love in your eyes
and for the very first time
i could see myself
a reflection of the person i am
and who i want to be

yes
you did that to me

what love does.

life with you
give me that
i want it forever
i've never felt something
more pure

the love you give.

love me like the stars

with you
love is simple

uncomplicated.

you rescued me
and put this aching heart
at ease

you are the answer.

remember when we were teens
and we would spend
countless hours on the phone
even then it wasn't enough
you had my heart
we were so in love
sneaking off to see each other
when our parents forbid it
endless laughing
creating memories
and throughout our adulthood
we always found our way back to one another
we were like two magnets
that couldn't stay away
and i am sure that when we are old
we will look back on our life
we will reminisce
and we will laugh
you will always be my dearest friend
no matter what
i am here for you
and i will love you
until the end

a.j.b.

me drinking coffee
on my balcony
eating bread with butter
reading my favorite book
wearing his t-shirt
the sun scorching against my skin
i wouldn't want it any different

glorious day.

love me like the stars

if rain be the sound of my love for you
then let it pour
let it drown the sky
let it storm
let the clouds gather and sing
let the ocean ride up onto the shore
let the wind howl
let it roar

that's how much
my heart beats out of my chest
that's how much
my love for you
is profoundly magnificent

he asked me how much i loved him.

this is my favorite page yet

with him.

love me like the stars

if you fall in love with me
you will live forever

in my stories.

let's breathe in this morning air
as the sun peeks in
and the rays are beaming
while our shadows dance on the ceiling
let's embrace this feeling

take my hand
let me help you trace
the shape
of my silhouette
and the details
that make it so wonderfully intricate

let's stay in bed a little while longer
wrapped in tangled sheets
lost in our tangled desires

let's make our own wildfire
that spreads with intensity
each and every time
you gaze at me

let's recite our love in poetry
in a language
that only you and i can speak

let's exist only in this moment
just you
unequivocally
loving every inch of me

lazy sunday's with you.

love me like the stars

he painted the moon
the sky
and the stars
as he gently whispered
through my eyes this is who you are

he sees beauty.

being with you
is an experience
i float
outside of my body
when in your presence

your love
makes me dance in ways
i never thought i could
and in all the ways
i knew i would

he loves me.

love me like the stars

can i stand in the sun with you
can you teach me
all of the ways
in which
i can hopelessly love you

apollo.

we co-existed
that's all there is to it

our fairytale.

love me like the stars

your love filled the void

whole.

do you promise to hold me close forever
because you make me better
you don't want me to be
what this tired world expects of me

you want me to be
love
to radiate love
to accept my flaws
to go after what i want

you want me to be
light
to be a reflection of light
to find beauty in my obstacles
to uplift and inspire

you make me better
because you want me to be
no one else
but the best version of myself

meteor shower.

love me
like the stars
and i'll be yours
always
and forever more

the beginning and the end.

heartache

before you grow
you will break

and sometimes
this is the best kind of
heartache

Bloom

the pain was too much to bear
my only choice was to write out
the voices in my head

heartache.

my past won't sleep
i wake up screaming from my dreams
the anxiety is choking me
i just want to rip out my heart
i don't want to feel so deeply anymore
the darkness is a cloud
that happily swallows me whole
i drown in my tears
give into my fears
while the ghosts
have made my soul eternally theirs

nightmare on earl street.

i'm scared i said
that's good he reassured
how i questioned
because it means you're still human

not completely broken.

when you left
time stood still
my limbs
were lifeless
you took my sun
you took my will
i ached for you
felt all of this pain for you
and for the moment
there is nothing else i can do

so here i lie
trying to manage
the delicate balance between
hating you
and loving you still

your absence.

love me like the stars

i was in love with you
because
you were a reflection
of the love i gave you

the mirror effect.

my feelings are hurt
my pride is in ruins
my heart is shattered
you were all that mattered
and you tore me apart
left me damaged in the dark

i thought forever
would be with you
but really
how could that be true
these things you can never know
so now i must learn
how to let you go

caged bird.

love me like the stars

i am in love with you
but you are in love with her
what do i do with this

move on
and pretend you don't exist
or allow you
to remain in my grasp
where i continue to hold on so tight
that my fingers
have no choice
but to bleed hopeless tears
while i wallow in my fears

i'm waiting for you to come
though deep down i know
you will never be here
to rid me of my sorrow

prelude to agony.

alesia carter

if you leave
don't come back
my heart is not a revolving door
for you to step out
and step back in

adieu.

love me like the stars

before you grow
you will break

and sometimes
this is the best kind of heartache

bloom.

you're supposed to be my someone
but instead
you break me down
into pieces
until i crumble
i suppose
i gave you the hammer
so i contributed to a fault

still
you didn't have to make me feel like
i am no one

bruised.

the monsters call me
i try not to answer
but they hide under my bed
and in my closet

they haunt my dreams
i run
i run
and i run
i can't escape
they keep pulling me back to yesterday

they trap me
put shackles on my ankles
the weight i can't bear
i am their prisoner
as they chew me slowly for dinner

they bring up things
that are conflicting
they want me
to live in angst
turmoil
devastation
and despair
they are drowning me in their misery
i desperately gasp for air

i try to imagine the light
that will allow me to get out of their sight
until finally
i found the courage to put up a fight
i faced those monsters
looked them straight in their eyes
told them to get ready for their demise
i frantically yelled with all my might
i relentlessly screamed in fright
but they just stood there
looking at me
ever so nonchalantly

with tears pouring down my face
i was taken aback
to sadly realize
they weren't so different
i saw the familiarity
the similarities
the aching
they were hurting
they were bleeding
i saw their open wounds

the monsters i saw
were the monsters
in me too

a monster's lullaby.

love me like the stars

he was my magic
and i loved every bit of his sorcery
even when
he was the reason
for my pain
and suffering

the wizard of my broken heart.

i try to dream up
the colorful moments
of what used to be
the cosmic love
that once was you and me
of the time i etched
the constellation into your skin
of the time that i could only exist
in your atmosphere

cosmos.

love me like the stars

buy me flowers
white roses
blush roses
shower me with their petals
they make everything better

band aid.

at the very least
be honest with me
aren't you sick and tired
of the lying

compulsive anguish.

love me like the stars

how can i be with you
but feel lonely in your presence
i reach out my hand
but you're in the distance

rearview mirror.

i've made numerous mistakes
i've done
what i consider to be
some horrible things
or maybe
that's the extreme thinking
of my shame

like a snake
i shed my skin
hoping to be born again

guilt.

love me like the stars

my heart is the ocean
and the waves
well
those are my emotions

soul.

hurt people
will hurt people
because they do not comprehend
that beyond the obstacle
or what makes us different
lays a hopeful chance
to be better humans
and so
they would rather be scared
stuck in the present
drowning in quicksand

comfort zone.

i was there for you
went above and beyond for you
shared my darkest
and most haunting secrets
because i thought i could be vulnerable
with you
you spoke so highly of good vibes
and positivity
that i thought you were my soul sister

i gave you my time
and my energy relentlessly
but instead
you are more loyal to those
who don't acknowledge your existence
have they done for you
the way that i did

my opportunity was your opportunity
but you left me in the trenches
to fend for myself
treated me like i am the help
as if i should've just been grateful
to merely be in your presence
but you took advantage

i genuinely supported you
i unselfishly looked out for you
you couldn't look out for me too
how can you say you're a friend
where have you been
while i've been drowning
in the deep end

maybe
you weren't the person
you claimed to be
maybe
i only mattered
because of what i could give

and what you could get
maybe
you never really wanted
to see me win

was it jealousy
was it insecurity
i don't understand
another lesson learned
where i've been burned
here we go again
even girl friends can be
just like
an unfaithful man

unsupportive friends.

how hard it must be
to live in a society
where you are condemned
and judged
based on who you love
how lonely it must feel
when you constantly hear
people would rather see
you have your rights denied
than to see you live with pride
how awful it must be
to be put down
to not be able to come out

you are not a sickness
or a disease
that needs to be cured
you don't need to be fixed
or convinced to experience
something different
you are a human
and you deserve
happiness

you are allowed to be who you want to be.

i weep for humanity
my heart breaks for the enslaved
a vicious cycle of crime opportunity
i weep for those
who never get their justice
for the mothers who have to bury their child
for other countries
where there is no end in sight to the wars
that are taking away their land
and bombing their homes
i weep for immigrants
who have to continuously prove
that they love their country
just as much as anyone born there would
i weep for those
who constantly have to fight to be heard
for those
who are subjected to
having their freedoms stripped
little by little
one by one
until there is nothing left to take anymore
if you are like me
to feel these things doesn't make you weak
it makes you a human being

lachrymose.

my heart is full of love
it has been stomped on
it has been ravished with pain
shattered and broken

and yet

my lungs still breathe in air
i still live
so that i may one day
love again

beautifully broken.

depression
social anxiety
a self-infliction of insecurities
sometimes it can be
more than i can bear
it's an overwhelming feeling
that clouds my judgement
in my weakest moments of despair

there were plenty of times
i felt like
i couldn't take it
that i couldn't manage
that i couldn't make it

how can i describe the distress

it's like losing a limb
it's becoming numb until you don't exist
it's feeling different from everyone else
it feels like you are invisible
that you are outside of yourself
it's being alone
as though
your gut is split open
and on display for the next show

and so i create
i create to take away the pain that gnaws and grows
i create to take away all that is insufferable
and it is my hope that reading this
helps you find comfort in my words
and peace within your world
but if you ever doubt your existence
please pick up the phone and speak your heart
until it heals

1 800 273 8255.

it's a funny thing
our need to explain
and to apologize for the times
we need a break
from society

do i have to post on social media today.

you are my equal
yet
they treat you
as if you're a different species
from out of this world
they vote to condemn you
but i say
be you
dance on your beautiful rainbow
if it makes your heart sing
who i am to judge your story
or your heart
who am i to take away your basic human rights
who am i to tell you who to love
that is far too much power for anyone

equality.

love me like the stars

i am tired of the impression
that anything black
is lesser than
that anything black
is not equivalent

unconscious prejudice.

i wasn't popular. i wasn't the prettiest girl. i was the girl everyone ignored. so i made the choice to create my life through pure alchemy. oh how revenge is so sweet.

unpopular.

i like to think that
it's not too late for me
that i'm still loveable
desirable
dateable
baggage and all
with my flaws
could he
whoever he may be
still love me

i have decided
that if love comes
i'll welcome it with open arms
and if it decides to leave
then i'll let it fly
because what is meant for me
will be for me
and i do not desire to keep
anything not for me

damaged goods.

i want a love so beautiful that i get lost
lost in his arms
lost in his eyes
lost in his heart
i just want to feel something
other than this numbness that is lingering
i want to know
that with him lying by my side
that just for a moment
i can forget the world
because all that exists
is him in mine

i want to love so much
that he becomes a piece of me
that he becomes the best part of me
i want to drown in his love
i want it to consume me
to wrap itself around me
to be a love that i've never felt before
i want it to be the kind of love
that saves me from myself
if but once more

evoke.

love me like the stars

don't just love the idea of me
love me for me
wholeheartedly
don't just want a taste
take me for all that i am
keep me safe
don't just want me for one thing
be my everything
don't just want me for the night
when i am deserving of the moon and the stars in the sky
don't let me just be a fantasy
i am deserving of more than your basic needs
if that's not something you can see
my darling
then you are not meant for me

i deserve to be loved.

i'm drowning
and sometimes
i can't get out of bed in the morning
while other days
i'm ready to conquer the world
but most days i hide away
with guilt eating at my sides
exposing my scars
i hate these marks
and what i see in the mirror
because the pain that looks back
becomes so much clearer

ashamed of my existence
my heart shattered into pieces
sometimes for no reason
because i can have it all
and still feel nothing at all
i can still feel alone and forsaken
i can be on top of the world
on the outside a success
but on the inside
i'm slowly dying
and crumbling

a chemical imbalance
or a tragic soul destined to be lost
the sadness is heavy
but i put on my mask
play the game
a daily masquerade

no one sees
the struggle
the hurt
the pain
the tears behind the smile
while
grief covers every part
of my dull aching body

i push through
because i have to
i stay strong in knowing
that there is purpose in my pain
to one day
be able to say
i'm
ok

depression part 1.

alesia carter

if only
i could love me
as much
as i love you

wounds.

maybe
just maybe
if i open up
you can show me who you are
maybe you will mend
all that is broken in my heart
maybe
just maybe
it's you
that will heal these scars
and put these pieces back together
that i so desperately cling to
maybe
we'll become one
and the pain i felt
will be gone
maybe
you'll take me away
to a place
where my soul
meets yours

in your grace.

i give so much to others
that i have nothing left for myself
but that always seems to be a woman's place
to give and give
sacrifice her needs
drowning mentally
exhausted bones
fed up emotionally
tired
drained
i just want to scream
my body hurts
i'm numb
incapable of rising
to the morning sun
there's this hurting
an uneasy feeling
the taste of loneliness
and the despair in realizing
i am alone
and that this broken heart
is my only home

half full.

love me like the stars

it comes in waves
the love
the pain

rollercoaster.

all of me
is
tired

consumption.

how do i begin to explain
how do i put into words
all of my pain
you should feel so lucky
to not feel what i feel
to not parade around
with this shame
with this guilt
i feel that i
have failed my child
where did i go wrong
is this my fault
or was he doomed
long before he was born
the same way that i was
life has always felt like my curse
could never really get ahead of the curve

it's so heavy
this feeling
it's a cloud that constantly
hovers over me
i want to be
the best mother i can possibly be
i want to mend
the broken fences
so that he knows
his mother
did not drown in her unspeakable sorrow

a mother's grief.

i was afraid of the dark
until i saw the stars shine
it was as though
they dried the tears from my weary eyes
a feeling of relief washed over my heart
and cleansed my bruised soul
i began to feel safe
it was a feeling i had never known

the stars
bathe me in their warmth
and encircle me in their light
the demons in my head
vanished from sight
i am finally
where i belong
i am no longer
alone

the girl that cried.

love me like the stars

the validation you seek
is already within your thoughts
turn to your heart
that's where you'll find
the one

reflection.

i thought it was my fault
i didn't realize what he did was wrong

silenced shame.

the truth has been hard to face
in a way
i have been living in denial
it has been difficult to admit
to my family and my friends
that i am silently suffering
from depression
it's not just waking up sad
it's a constant feeling bad
a void
a hole so shallow
that when i extend my arms
there is no one to help
there is only my shadow
to swallow me whole
to eat the flesh
from my rotting bones

depression part 2.

i am so very
deeply
incredibly
truly
sorry
for the pain
you've had to endure
it isn't fair
i know

empathy.

i like to be alone
i've always been alone
it is how i recharge and reset
it is how i find meaning
i'm not interested
in being one of the cool kids
please do not take offense
when i say
let's get coffee
yet you don't see me again
i'm not trying to be a flake
it's just that
each day is a different struggle for me
my social anxiety
is a weight attached to my legs
but also
being alone gives me solace
it makes me happy
it gives me comfort
i like my life private
i just ask
that you respect that
that you get that
instead of misunderstanding
and making your own assumptions
about who i am

anti-social.

the gut-wrenching truth is that
sometimes
love is temporary
enjoy it now
in this moment
knowing that it is to help you grow
cherish your happiness
soak in it
appreciate it
be grateful for it
as you are grateful for the morning sun
because even if this feeling
this love
fades away
it doesn't mean that it is the end
my darling
you will experience
great love once again

loving and healing.

love me like the stars

the sun sets
and it will rise again
whether or not
you are there

the absence of you.

when we met
we were just teenagers
i was feeling damaged
and broken
i wasn't just alone
i was lonesome
a loner
an outsider looking in
i know you felt just as different
my pain matched yours
and that's what made us work
i stood by you
no matter what wrong you did
i thought that's what love meant

you needed me
and i was ready to serve
the only thing that mattered
was what you deserved
i gave and i gave
i somehow became
a mother role instead
the countless sacrifices i made
were always for you
you never did the same for me too

and so years later
when we had our first born son
i never thought that after all i had done
you would willingly leave me for another woman
when i had been the one
to build you up
with every ounce of love
i had in my bones
but you left me alone

we didn't have very many problems
other than struggling to make ends meet
as we lived in poverty

so i don't understand
what made you think
it was ok to walk away from me
without hesitancy

my heart was in pieces
yet
i yelled after you
with tears in my eyes
crying
come back home
please don't go
but still
you got in the car with her
you drove off
she convinced you to leave us behind
she stole you
like a thief in the night
convinced you
you were hers
and not mine
she was a criminal
that purposely tore us apart
and now
you are angry at me
angry for not waiting
for not loving you
the way i used to
believe me i tried
but while you were gone
at some point in time
i realized
you were no longer the air i needed to survive

it's unfortunate
that your anger for me
far exceeds
the love for your child
who is in need of you more than i

how could you be an absent father
how do you go on about your day
without a bother
how do you sleep at night
how do you live
knowing you abandoned him
and have done little to reach out
to ask him to forgive your sins

don't you remember
when your parents
abandoned you
so how could you put him through
the same thing too
forget your love for me
i don't want it
and you shouldn't want it either
that time has come and gone
if you love me
really love me
you will love your son
and give him the opportunity
to know a father's love

g.l.s.

i have accepted
that there will be highs
and that there will be lows
lots of lows
that may feel like
i am ready to explode
i feel deeply
it's just how i was made
i'm an emotional wreck
i wear my heart on my sleeve
sometimes i'm an imperfect
but beautiful mess
and yet
i wouldn't change a damn thing
about who i am

sensitive.

here's to
endless kisses
late night conversations
that led to morning sunrises
you buying me a bouquet
of my favorite flowers
adventures and laughs
rainy days wrapped in your arms
as the record player played our song
how could we have shared
something so beautiful
for you to turn out
so unbelievably wrong

these are my memories of you.

love me like the stars

you disrespect me
because you don't see my value
if i have to convince you of my worth
you don't deserve my presence

ungrateful.

we fell fast and hard
it was lust
not love
i guess that's why
it all went wrong
i don't know what i was thinking
i just knew you made me feel good
at a time when i needed love
and had no one to count on

things got complicated
heated and messy
you abandoned me
left me stranded for dead
on the inside
i might as well have been

those wounds cut so deep
i bled mentally
i quivered at the knees
i struggled to cope
me and this child of yours
that i carried for nine months
i remember the call
in which you told me
that isn't my baby
just like to you deny deny deny
we were not a concern to you
you easily moved on with your life
left us behind so you could get yourself a wife

you put me through
the worst kind of pain
you were less than two miles away
and i lived in a shelter
with not even a penny to my name
i was at my lowest point ever
it was truly the definition
of rock bottom

love me like the stars

and on the day
that my water would break
i specifically
remember the call
when you told me to hold on
you hung up on me
i didn't exist to you
you purposely left
your phone off the hook
because i had no other way to reach you
that you knew

it was like my breath left my body
to see that
even in that moment
you treated me
and your newborn baby like nobodies
you were a real life form of a savage
that caused my utterly bruised soul havoc

over the next few years
you fell in my grace
yet continued to be a disgrace
sending my photos to your ex
while laughing behind my back
spreading secrets
exposing my flaws
that i am most certainly not proud of
those were not your stories to tell
you in my life was literal hell
i couldn't catch a break
from the exhausting
and overwhelming distress
you continued to inflict with your hate
admittedly i wasn't exactly innocent
i was filled with rage
i was young and naive
how could i allow you in
to hurt me again and again
and again

you stomped on my heart
because to you
i was no one
you thought i was worthless
respect was not associated with my name
you spat on it
you took advantage
fed me with lies
to keep me full
you had the most loveliest disguise
of them all though

i made my mistakes
i made my bed
and had the unfortunate experience
of lying in it
i came to grips
with my haunting past
so forgive me
if i choose to keep
my distance from your wrath
if i choose to not take your call
if i choose not to think of you at all
if i choose to not befriend
the woman who kicked me
when i was on the ground suffering
while you idly stood by
to watch my fall and clap at my demise

still somehow
i continued to rise
and now
i am at peace
because overcoming you
was one of my greatest victories

don't fret
you weren't my biggest regret
because i have

the sweetest little boy
who loves me
who gives me hugs
who watches over me
like an angel sent
from the heavenly skies above
you played no part in that
my son was born
out of the love *i* had

the book of david.

he's a man
should not be an excuse
to justify
his every wrongdoing

disguised misogyny.

love me like the stars

you are my sister
why would i find relief and pleasure
in your failure

i am not your enemy.

i think back on myself
as a little girl
and i shed a tear
for my innocence
that would soon be broken
she didn't deserve to be hurt
but it's an odd thing
life that is
it takes you down a path
some good
some bad
and in the end
it's all about
perspective

dark matter.

i used to think
that my hair defined me
that if i straightened it
i would look pretty
i must admit
i still struggle with this concept
i used to think
that if i got plastic surgery
to fix my nose
that i would look prettier in photos
i used to think
that if i could just get rid of my stretch marks
i would be more appealing
i used to think
that if i got rid of my acne scars
that would mean i was more beautiful
i choose to expose
my insecurities
to show that we all have complexities
and awkward tendencies
but absolutely none of these
define me

insecure.

i used to be ashamed
of the body i have
these hips
these breasts
i covered them in baggy clothes
as to not fill the shape of me in them
my only defense was to be a tomboy
collect baseball cards and comic books
my mother thought i was a lesbian
she never thought to think
talk to your daughter about her growing body
we dare not have those conversations
i had to learn on my own
mistake after mistake
after mistake
until those lessons were well learned

what i didn't learn from my mother.

it's such a small
and frivolous thing
to think
that i can stand on my porch
without fear of torture
that i can have a home
in a beautiful place
without fear
that it will be invaded
that i can close my eyes
and smell the fresh air
as i listen
to the sounds of birds chirping
i can hear them sing
thank god
i am free
but
a sadness casts over me
because
this feeling
was supposed
to be
everyone's
american dream

freedom.

i was born with struggle
the color of my skin
determines my experiences
because our country is plagued with racial bias
and so i know
to speak up
is a complex inner battle
sometimes it's not always simple
not everyone has the courage
but i was not granted the luxury
to simply stand indifferent
while these topics are uncomfortable
they must be said and shared
it's time we face
the truth about injustice and prejudice
it's my reality
and the reality of countless others
we cannot water down the truth
to cater to you
take the time
to try and understand
what systematic oppression is
if one calls you out
don't be offended
eat the words you've been served
digest the words
and evaluate your stance
you may just see
how you contribute to society
whether knowingly or unconsciously

the miseducation of white privilege.

love me like the stars

you are successful at being everything and anything
other than yourself

fake.

the money   means nothing
the material things   mean nothing
the popularity
the conformity
selling my soul
for a couple thousand likes or more
just for you to like me
all   mean nothing
it's empty
that world means nothing to me
but some like you
may thrive on the hypocrisy

to stand up for what's right
means something
to speak up
even if my tongue feels heavy
means something
to use my influence
if only to make a small difference
means something

your silence
makes the ground shake
it speaks so loudly
i cannot bear the sound
choosing to stay silent
means everything
and does nothing

superficiality.

i wasn't the girl
who had a lot of friends
i have always marched
to my own beat
creating my opportunity
not waiting on anything
'til this day
i couldn't tell you
that i have a best friend
i haven't been
able to depend
on anyone
to be around
too many disappoints
you let them in
they let you down
i think now
i realize
my destiny is different
my purpose is bigger
it may not reflect
what you expect
but i am ok
knowing that

friends are overrated.

verse 1
when i wake up in the morning
have to get my fix
i'm addicted to you
without you i'm so sick
you're bad for my blood
i'm sure ~~i know~~ i'll suffer for this
but i'm not thinking of the consequences
just what my heart is feeling

hook 2x
love and drugs
sometimes they feel like one in the same
love and drugs
you're like the poison in my veins
love and drugs
need something to numb this pain
love and drugs
can't let love take me out this way

verse 2
you were sweet for a moments time
then suddenly
you were awful to me
it ~~was~~ was too late before i realized
we weren't meant to be
i was too in love and blind to see
that my lover and my best friend
was my own worst enemy
you pulled my heart's strings
but you'll always be my baby
like my favorite song
that you played for me
shattered me into pieces
but i'll be just fine
even if you're no longer mine

repeat hook 2x

verse 3

sometimes i miss the sound of your guitar
but i no longer know who you are
it was perfect on the surface
but inside we were both hurting
falling so deep so fast
i saw the signs in front of my face
thought it was just a test of my faith
but i ignored the feeling
the truth is that not everything is what it seems
the arguments / the lies / the betrayal
you took apart of me
when i gave you everything
and in the end to you it meant nothing

hook 2x
love and drugs
sometimes they feel like one in the same
love and drugs
you're like poison in my veins
love and drugs
need something to numb this pain
love and drugs
can't let love take me out this way

bridge
amnesia amnesia
sometimes i wish i had amnesia amnesia
because then i wouldn't need you need you
amnesia amnesia
i wish i had amnesia amnesia
then i wouldn't need you need you

repeat until fade out

a.c.: heartbreak song.

heartbreak
is nothing new to me
in a way
it has become
my only friend

mr. reliable.

i never told you how i felt about you
mostly because i was terrified of rejection
i didn't want to face
whether you had the same sentiments
if you did
it meant i had to be whole and honest
if you didn't
i had to face the fact that really
i didn't belong in your world

and so i settled
i settled for half of you
let you have half of me too
you were so special to me
you were kind and sweet
the night we met was like out of a dream
we were at venice beach
i was feeling insecure
but i felt like the luckiest girl
that's when you kissed me for the first time
under a sky full of dimly lit stars
and when in that moment you smiled afterwards
you had me
that was it
my heart was yours

for a moment
i believed we could be something beautiful
it didn't matter
that we were two countries apart
it was better like that for us both
to remain unavailable
i could adore you from a distance
be proud of your accomplishments
there was no wrong you could do
except when i flew to see you
but i didn't see you
you left me hanging
worst yet
you didn't say sorry

i never said so
but
i need you to know
that hurt me
that cut my soul
it woke me up from my fantasy
finally
i accepted reality
you could never love someone like me
i would never be whole with you
it wasn't in the cards
and that was further confirmed
when i saw a picture of her
a blonde
she was the complete opposite of me
she fit in your world
more than i ever could
that broke me
still i told you
i was happy you found someone
that made you happy
even though the girl
i wanted you to be happy with
was me

s.p.: a canadian romance.

love me like the stars

i didn't know you
but i am hurting for you
hurting so bad
that it's as if you were my own son
your story breaks my heart
i cannot fathom the feeling of losing a child
when it could have been prevented
but our system is broken
and no one cares to fix it
i grieve for you
i wish we could have crossed paths
i wish i could have given you kindness
to reassure you that you were loved
that there was hope for a better tomorrow

and at night
i cry for you
uncontrollably
if only there was something
anything
that i could have done
to ease your pain and suffering

i am so sorry
that they treated you wrong
that the bullying hurt
your gentle eight-year-old soul
that you thought your life
wasn't worth fighting for

you deserve to be living
to be laughing
to feel happy
you deserve better
you deserve justice
and to your mother
my sincerest condolences

gabriel taye.

you pick on others
and are selfishly mean
you may even push and pull
laugh in their face
make fun of their clothes
their nose
their hair
the color of their skin

your words hurt
they cut like a sword
they create damage
that can be irreparable
are you so consumed with hate
and negativity
that you are ok living with this reality

i believe you are hurting
projecting your feelings
because anything is better
than facing your demons
but no matter how old you are
a child or adult
you must be a better person
a person who shows compassion
for the differences in us humans

a letter to bullies.

there has to be
something beyond the surface
there are so many people hurting
are you not angry
do you not feel
do you not see
what is happening in the world
where is your compassion
where is your heart
what makes you think
that this isn't your problem to help solve
we are all connected
that's the way it works
don't tell me you stand idle
as to not ruffle any feathers
because
what's wrong is wrong
what's right is right
we must stand together
we must fight

i don't understand your silence.

pain
anguish
tears of sadness
shame
darkness
demons
defiance
i succumb to the same battles
feeling broken down
feeling alone
unpretty
unworthy
abandoned
drowning in sorrow
like there's no tomorrow
our hearts beat the same
i am like you
you are never alone
i hurt like you too

i hope you find peace in your heart.

love me like the stars

share
like
follow
comment
aren't you tired of it

there is more to life.

do something

    do something

        do something

what can i do.

love me like the stars

i will not stand down
i will not let you slander my culture
to fulfill your propaganda
that paints a picture
of black lives that don't matter
emotionless and cruel
white supremacy will never rule

how can you kill another black boy
and try to justify
that he was a thief
a no good thug
that got what he deserved

say his name

how can you claim
she took her own breath away
when she stood for fighting
and lived for the truth

say her name

why didn't you give him a fighting chance
guns drawn and with no hesitation
bam bam

say his name

a hood didn't mean he was dangerous
my heart aches for his innocence

say his name

he was reaching for his wallet
no harm no foul
but instead you rang fire

say his name

the pain
the pain
the pain
explain
explain
explain
the truth
we demand the truth

you claim he was holding a gun
how is it that you couldn't identify
what it really was
your lies
are drenched in blood
and it leads to no convictions
where is the justice
for the countless families
that have to unnecessarily suffer

this is why we march
this is our resilience
this is why we protest
this is why we chant
black lives matter
until our voices crack

injustice.

love me like the stars

you don't understand
because you lack empathy

reality check.

when i find my voice
i am ignored
when i speak
i am looked at
as no good
so i write these words
knowing you have no choice but to listen
do you hear me now
or shall i speak louder
until your bones shake

will you then
finally accept me

when the thunder rolls in.

love me like the stars

so desperate to fit in
without actually wanting to be the best
or wanting to make a difference
the narcissistic self interest
is severely clouding your judgment

popularity.

my entire life
i have felt like i am not enough
not enough to be someone who is loved
why would i be the girl
that any man could want
not enough to be someone's friend
what could i possibly possess
that would make me like her her or her
i suppose
i am far too different
i don't fit a certain image
even when i am kind
i am stabbed in the front with no hesitance

always overlooked
is my life story
but i am tired
so tired of being disregarded
simply because
my skin doesn't blend in
and i don't have a certain status like popularity
i am tired
so tired
of you disrespecting me

just wait and see
i am going to be
everything
you never thought
i could be
i will be everything i have ever dreamed
because
i believe in me

enough.

admit that
sometimes you are fake
and smile in someone's face
even when you are ridden
with jealousy and hate

fake friends.

why is it easier for a man to walk away
why is it ok for him
to not show strength
to not show restraint

it is unacceptable
for the burdens to fall on a woman
for her to be the one
to find the more sensible solution

she is always the one
to pick up the grief-stricken pieces
that the men in her life
have selfishly broken

single mother.

do i have to get dressed today
are pajamas and slippers ok
do i have to wear make-up today
to cover up my imperfections and scars
that are a reflection of the weight on my heart
do i have to put a smile on my face today
so no one can see the hurt in my eyes
and the pain that is beyond
that gently tears me apart
do i have to pretend
that my life is magnificent
instead of coming to terms with my sadness

one
two
three days
a week goes by
and i'm still feeling the same way inside
i'm still pondering the same questions
for which i have no answers

do i
do i
do i

depression part 3.

stand with me
close your eyes
breathe in the fresh air

do you hear
the birds singing
do you feel
the breeze

can you feel
the sun kissing your skin
can you taste
the salty ocean

can you hear her
whispering
gently weeping
pleading
to take care
of what we have

mother earth.

love me like the stars

i'm trying to find peace
but life has me falling to my knees
one disaster after another has broken me
how can this be reality
why we do we lack empathy
party over people
profits over people
power over people
party over country
it's disgusting

how are we human beings
without reflecting
the true definition
of what it means
to be human
why do we teach hate to our children
why do we force them to carry the burden of despair
when we know the answer
is and always will be clear

love will dissipate the hate
love will heal our hearts
love will turn grass green
and make flowers bloom
love is in me
and i truly believe
love is in you too

dona nobis pacem.

black is dirty
white is purity
brown is just as bad as black
how absurd is that

fake news.

love me like the stars

they do not like me
because my skin is brown
they do not respect me
because my skin is brown
they do not take me seriously
because i am brown

their hate
their disgust
their prejudice
their ignorance
is unjust
it gives a false sense of superiority among us

on the contrary
being different
makes me pretty incredible
because
you take
you want
you want my brown skin
you want my lips
you want my ass
you want my hips
you want my hourglass shape
you want my culture
because it's cool
it's like honey
addicting and sweet
it lacks no substance
it's light-years beyond your mere comprehension

you take
you want
yet you can't use your voice to speak up

the only time black culture rules
is when the profits hit your wallet
or when you obsess over beyoncé and rap artists

when we need you
you shrink like a coward
while you claim *that's not my problem*

you take
you want
it never stops

we are degraded and gunned down
simply because we are colored
the burdens we take and tolerate
the weight we hold on our shoulders
and carry on our backs
literally and figuratively
somehow
we can turn it into something magnificent
despite your hate
we will rise above
your empty shallowness

we are constantly overlooked
and disrespected
our talents
and contributions
are underappreciated

you would prefer
we stay silent
but that won't happen
the capabilities we have
are multifaceted
the faith we have
you can't touch it
we are strong
i am strong
we are resistant
i am resistant
we are intelligent
we are not apprehensive

we are proud
black
latina
african american
puerto rican
this is my heritage
this is my history
we are an undeniable beauty

we
are
royalty

being brown in america.

we will not be silenced
we will not be oppressed
build a wall
and we will find a way to climb it
don't you dare claim the word of god
or even speak his name
when you put on the devil's costume
and proudly walk in shame

mr. president.

i began writing
and i couldn't stop writing
the words
that were once hidden
locked and buried away
they found their way
and made their escape
they were fighting
because they knew
they needed to be said

oh honey
it's going to be
one hell of a reckoning

the truth will come to light.

love ~~xxx~~ ain't for me

verse 1
i haven't been so lucky in love
and it's getting tough
because i crave a love so deep
to simply touch me
i don't want to give all of me
without it meaning a thing
i don't want a fling
i want him to be my one love, my baby

hook
it's such a sad thing but i'm starting to think
that love just ain't for me
because if it was
why does it hurt so much?
love just ain't for me
i guess it's just not in the cards
because it always falls apart
maybe one day (one day)
love will be for me

verse 2
they say be patient
they say it'll come when you're not looking
but see i don't look
they come and go
even though i ~~xxx~~ give my all and some more
one after one
how can they all be wrong?
so sick of sad love songs
i did everything i was supposed to do
because isn't that what good people do?
so why
can't i have my happy ending too?

repeat hook

verse 3

how can one be so in love with love
you'd think it'd be easy
but it ain't so easy at all
and ▨▨ it breaks my heart
everytime i see someone
who has someone
it makes me bitter
because i'd give anything
for that special kind of feeling
why can't i have someone
who accepts my soul▨
who gives me their all
instead pain is my art
and it's the reason for this song

hook
it's such a sad thing
but i'm starting to think
that love just ain't for me
because if it was
why does it hurt me so much?
love just ain't for me
i guess it's just not in the cards
because it always falls apart
maybe one day (one day)
love will be for me

bridge
if only i could be happy
i just want to be happy
if only love was for me
instead pain is my art
and time after time
i watch it all fall apart
love ain't for me

it's just not in the cards / but i want my happy ending too

in this life
you will come across difficult
and sometimes cruel paths
the world will try to break you
and you may just end up broken
they will try to make you feel like
you don't belong
they are wrong
you belong

your faith
your courage
your strength
they can't take that away

the other side of the rainbow.

love me like the stars

you were the mother i didn't have
you taught me strength
you taught me resilience
you taught me how to be
the woman i am today
and for that
i am grateful
i am indebted to you

i wish i could have known you better
as a woman yourself
there was so much more for me to learn
i didn't think there could ever be
a world without you in it

you were majestic
a black unicorn
rare and precious
i never believed it was possible
that you could just not be here
when you were there for 31 years of my life
and at the blink of an eye
you died
i know you were tired
but i wish
you had held on for a little bit longer
your family still needed your guidance
and i still needed my grandmother

you had a heart of gold
you loved me beyond comprehension
even during the times i didn't deserve it
i wish had had more time
to be the granddaughter
that i should have been

on the day you passed
i regret not answering the phone
what would have been your last words
would you tell me

that i deserved god's blessings
that i deserved to be happy
that you loved the boys and me
that you had a feeling
that day
was going to be the day
that you took your last breath

grandmother
i am so sorry
for all of the things that i didn't do
but i find comfort in knowing
you are watching over me
i pray that you are at peace
and i just hope
that you would be proud of me

dear grandmother.

you were my idol
i put you on a pedestal
we were close
i so dearly loved you with all of my heart
we were almost a picture perfect family
i remember the days when we were normal
celebrating holidays in new york
doing things together every weekend
i remember when you cried
after hearing uncle curly died
i remember celebrating our birthdays
because i was born two days after yours
a leo father and his leo daughter
a lion and his cub
i remember the trips to shinders
you let me get comic books
and baseball cards like my brother
i remember when you would play with us
you were so fun
a father and his children
it was normal until it was foreign
i remember the paper route
the early mornings we would wake up
it was not the ideal job
but there was never a day
you didn't work hard
and that's where you laid the foundation
that taught me many lessons
that taught me to chase my dreams
to have a strong work ethic
and to never believe that i wasn't capable
of accomplishing anything
that the words *i can't* didn't belong in my vocabulary
i can't imagine what it's like
to be a black man
living in a white world
i imagine there's a lot of pressure

especially when you are young
and i'm sure
there was a lot of temptation
because the next memory is my least favorite
it was when the normalcy ended
it was when my mother died inside
it was when the little girl i was
started to hurt for the very first time
i remember the fight
the chaos
the yelling
i didn't know what it was
i don't remember the words
but i remember
watching in horror
as i was crying and confused
i remember my mother
taking glass from the coffee table
and slamming it into pieces
as she was desperately screaming
and you
you walked out
just like that
you walked away
from everything we had
that was when
i learned the definition of sad
little did i know i would one day experience
the same kind of pain and brokenness like she had
i wish i could say
things weren't that different
after you chose to leave
but my mother
was no longer loving
she was hurting
and that meant we silently suffered

love me like the stars

i do remember the times
when you were there
like at my sixth grade ski trip
my eighth grade graduation
and when you
bought me my first bike for my 10th birthday
things weren't all bad
but i still remember the times
i needed you
i would call and call
you wouldn't answer
i would wait and wait
you wouldn't show up for your daughter
i felt we were mostly forgotten
were you ashamed of us
the black and hispanic kids you had
because i remember
the women
that commanded your attention instead
and later the other kids you had
you started a new life
without me
without us in it
you never took me to disneyland
or on vacations
but it was your routine with them
and their extended family members
how could you give so much more to them
and leave us struggling
i never really thought that was fair
i was your second child
and suddenly we didn't matter
it left me with a feeling of abandonment
a feeling i would continue to battle
just know that it made me stronger
it made be better
it made me independent

father
i do not blame you
i am not angry at you
i know you can't say just how much
that you may be hurting
from your mistakes and your past
i can't speak on your regrets
but i look back
and i know you tried your best
with what you had
i know you would
give me everything
because you have
and i know on you
i can always depend

dear father.

i wish i could say
i had better memories
i wish i could say
we were close
and best friends
but the reality is
when we were kids
you made my life a living hell
you were always so angry
so bitter
rotten to the core
drenched with pain
your misery loved company
and you made sure i joined
my clearest memory is that
you were so mean
you were supposed to protect me
instead you punched me
pushed me
shoved me
called me ugly
damaged my heart
and my soul
in a way
that you will never know
you were supposed to look out for me
be the example
instead you left me behind
to live the fast life
i know this isn't entirely your fault
our parents weren't parents
they were absent
and left us
to figure things out on our own
our father wasn't there
to teach you how to be a man
our mother succumbed
to her depressive mood swings
i know these realizations
haunt you
just as much as they haunt me too

i am sorry for the pain you've had
to endure
and that no one was there
like they should have been for you
i am sorry
you had the short end of the stick
a life that
even up until now
feels cursed and forsaken
but isn't it funny
how life works
the tables have turned
now i am the one you need
now you need my sympathy
the good in me
wants to help
but something in me
resents you for the past
regardless
i will do the best i can
to be a sister that's there
i truly hope
you find your way
and i pray
you find your peace
and that you receive
endless blessings

dear brother.

you had us young
and i know it was hard
you didn't get to do
all that you dreamed of
you have yet to have
your picture perfect romance
the white dress
the wedding
or the white picket fence
maybe you could have had that
had we not been a burden
for a long time
i just didn't understand
the reasons why you did or said
the things you did
until i was eighteen
you had been so incredibly mean
i carried the thought
that my mother didn't like me at all
it was normal in our family to not talk
there was no communication
no expression of emotions
that was forbidden
there were no hugs or kisses
no i love you's or how was your day
you could never say
the things i so desperately needed
my mother to say
i had to navigate my own way
and discover my own mistakes
i know you carried a lot of pain
especially the day
my father walked away
i know life had broken your heart
and maybe
that's why you took it out on us

maybe that would explain
why your presence was more of a ghost
but what explains you turning an eye
when my brother
abused me mentally and emotionally
why did you let him hit me
didn't you see i was hurting
i spent my childhood living in turmoil
i had no one at home
but those trials and tribulations
made me who i am
i read books and i dreamed
i wrote songs and poetry
in order to cope with my problematic reality
i imagined a different life
in order to deal with my strife
if there was one thing i knew
i didn't want to be the mother that was you
yet somehow
i see parts of you in me too
i realize
i still have healing to do
because sometimes i get angry
when i think of the little girl
that suffered in silence
that cried in anguish
that didn't understand
what was happening
the little girl
that needed guidance
that only her mother
could have provided

dear mother.

love me like the stars

i hope you find comfort in your skin
and discover all of the love that you hold within

you are capable.

salvation

shame
anger scared
depression
guilt empty
frustration
unlovedy
unfair ugly

unpopular sadness
struggle regret hurt
confused
hopeless
alone despair

my tongue danced

the lump in my throat disappeared

the words dripped from my mouth

after thirty-three years of captivity

they were desperate

to be

free

love me like the stars

your past is not your prison
stop laying your head there to rest

salvation.

my tongue danced
the lump in my throat disappeared
the words dripped from my mouth
after thirty-three years of captivity
they were desperate to be free

liberated.

love me like the stars

if you see beauty in you
you will see beauty around you too

a rose without thorns.

if you are broken
you do not have to stay broken

it is your choice
to pick up the pieces
and move on

or live in a constant state of affliction
blaming others
for all of the wrong

choice.

let me tell you something about fear
it will blind you
it will misguide you
it will convince you
no you shouldn't do that
it will stop you in your tracks
it will suffocate you
until there is no life left
don't let fear hold you back
from chasing your dreams
from being all that you want to be
because you are never too young
or too old to adapt and change

fear will take over your gut
it will convince you
to do things
you shouldn't have done
or it will tell you to not even bother
because what good
could you possibly bring about
fear will make you push good souls away
it will outwardly take
your right to be happy
and sometimes it will bring pain

in the end
you must listen to your heart
that's where you start
because ultimately
fear is a choice
it resides only in your thoughts

the evolvement of fear.

i don't want to be realistic
optimistic yes
i want to crush negativity
i want to be free
to dream
the most extravagant
enchanting
magical
life i could lead

i want to break glass ceilings
not stoop to mediocrity
fit in or conform
that's not me
that's not where i belong

i am better than that.

i like strange
it's comforting

i like depth
substance

i like emotion
genuine souls
unafraid of feeling
and creating
that's what i relate to

surround me
with people like that
and i will feel whole

authentic.

alesia carter

let me see your scars
i think they are beautiful

vulnerable.

women are powerful
if we could
we would find a way
to move mountains
we show compassion
through action
we love
even when we break
we feel
even if our lives are at stake
we carry and birth life
and that life feeds from the food
our bodies create
how can that be anything
other than stunning

how can they try to belittle us
to demean our contribution
simply because they are scared
that in actuality
we are goddesses
that reign far superior

men need us
without us
they will wilt and wither
we are their rib
their seed is useless
without our uterus to plant it

so the next time a man
tells you to find your place
tell him to remember
the belly he came from
that the life he was given
was not without sacrifice
that misogyny has no place
they cannot take away women's rights

oh how he quickly forgets
he would not be here
had it not been for
the woman
who carried him

the crown that we wear.

love me like the stars

i am most at peace during the night
when all is calm
when all is still
yet you can hear the wolves

i am most myself in the darkness
there is a certain mystery
it is where i find wonder
it is where this lion finds her comfort

leave me to gaze at the moon
to be one with the stars
away from the madness and chaos

introverted leo.

so we meet again
how i've missed you
forgive me
for ever leaving you

ode to my pen and paper.

how to create your own happy

1. take a walk and treasure the fresh air

2. love and radiate love

3. don't go on social media today

4. write out your heart and your thoughts

5. speak only good things and repeat positive affirmations

6. read a book and feel the pages in-between your
   fingers because it's a special type of feeling

7. practice forgiveness and kindness and empathy

8. buy yourself flowers

9. learn something new about yourself or someone else

10. live in this very moment

selflessness is an indication
that one can deeply love

cogitation.

my experiences
have simply humbled me
they have taught me
to practice empathy

above all
it has softened me
rather than harden me

rewarding.

you are not them
you are not them
you
are
not
them

a gentle reminder.

i want to be surrounded by gorgeous watercolors of art and stars painted so beautifully that i feel like i'm losing myself in a wonderland.

the beauty of imagination.

alesia carter

if it feels scary
there's a pretty good chance you should do it
because all of the magic happens
outside of your comfort zone
never in it

risk.

love me like the stars

we talked
we laughed
how sweet you are
how genuine

i am thankful
our souls got to meet
let's do this again
over coffee

human connection.

alesia carter

rest
reset
it's ok
to
take it easy
today

breathe.

love me like the stars

unless you were me
or unless i decided to share
the most intimate parts of my past
you would not otherwise know
my life
or my struggles

wisenheimer.

thank you for believing in me
it was the greatest gift
you could give

gratitude.

love me like the stars

my dearest baby boy
you and your brother
are my joy
everything i do
i do it for you two

you see
i have made some mistakes
but i have never been ashamed
of the sacrifices i have had to make
even when i struggled
there was not one single regret
because the obstacles were worth it

you have comforted me
in times of sadness
in the midst of madness
when i cry
you cry
your heart is so kind
as you get older
please remember this
never apologize
for what you're feeling
your sensitivity is a strength
not a weakness

and of course
you must always know
that your mother loves you
ever so much

dear jaden.

my oldest son
it has been an honor
to see you grow
to see you blossom

i am sorry
i wasn't always
the mother you deserved
i was never good at hugs and kisses
and i know sometimes i didn't listen
i am sorry
for the pain i put you through
that wasn't fair
for me to do that to you
you are so strong and resilient
i know in my heart
that the future you hold
will be bright and beautiful

and most of all
i am sorry that
your father has not been there
that he hasn't realized
just how much he is missing
but i promise you one thing
i will always be here
the one you can count on to care
this is my vow to you
i will always
always
and forever
love you

dear trey.

love me like the stars

don't ask me to suppress
my thoughts and my feelings
to appeal to the masses
don't compare me or tell me
you sound like her
you sound like him
no
i am my own voice
and they are theirs
this journey is mine
it is not yours his or hers

i have been writing
since i was five years' old
this is my right
this is my heart
this is my journey
whether you like my words or not

my poetry
the ugly
the pretty
and all that is in-between
is an extension of me
that fills up the insides of me
to bring out the depths in me
i will not be ashamed of my story
that has brought me so much glory

if for me to appease
is what you want
i am not sorry to say
you've got the wrong one

enlightenment.

if you are comfortable
with being alone
that is when you can truly love
because if by chance your heart breaks
when he or she walks away
then
at least
you
will stay

you are not a condition of the other.

my past does not define me
my mistakes mean i am human
and sometimes i will make them
so do not condemn
the person i used to be
that person is no longer me

adaptation.

this is my choice
who are you to take it away from me

free will.

love me like the stars

just in case you forgot
or didn't know
you
matter
and always
will

don't let the world determine your ending.

alesia carter

it's a long journey to acceptance
it takes courage

may you learn to love
the broken
and most unbeautiful pieces

being comfortable in your own skin.

love me like the stars

i do not believe that
the universe will punish you
for not knowing how to love yourself
i do not believe that
you will be damned

i believe
the universe will bring you someone
who can teach you how to love
over and over again

we are not perfect beings.

she's a woman
what do you expect
her hormones
control her emotions
she's fat
she's ugly
she's lazy
she's crazy
she's belligerent
she's vindictive
how can you trust her
she belongs in the kitchen
crucify her at the stake
hunt her like the witch she is

do you see what's wrong here
pitting women against women
to create destruction
to shut us down
from gaining power

because if we're too distracted
with hating one another
there's no way we can discover
the courage we can muster
to fight for our rights
and take back control
to protest and to tell the men
hell   no

tabloids.

i will not apologize
for not fitting your standard of beauty
but i will recommend
finding a new lens
and maybe
you will find
an altered
definition

unapologetically me.

write your story
breathe it
live it
manifest it

mantra.

a man doesn't validate me
he doesn't give me an identity
he doesn't define me
on the contrary
he compliments me
in the ways i allow it to be
because even without him
i am golden
i am happy
i am still me

individualistic.

you've changed they say
as if
i am supposed to have struggled
be flat broke
and still say the same
no
that is growth
i will not forget where i came from
but i will not apologize
for my blessings
when my future was already written

do not judge my journey.

love me like the stars

stop comparing yourself to others
you've endured far too much
to not acknowledge your own progress

you are your own goals.

speak your truth
be your truth
walk in your truth

unconventional.

love me like the stars

with little to no representation
how could i have otherwise known
that the innocent beautiful girl i was
could grow up to make a difference in this world

dear little mixed girl.

your pain
is your purpose

while the burden
is only for a season
remember
it is always
always
for a reason

own your story.

show up
even when it's hard
even when you can't take it anymore
even if you have to do
things you don't necessarily
want to do
show up
because there are no shortcuts
or a fast track
you must go through it
in order
to come out
the other side
a success

resilience.

i think
the most important thing you can do
is choose people
who freely
choose you

invest your energy wisely.

how have we lost the concept
of human connections
and real authentic relationships
how have we lost
what it means
to be emotionally intelligent
we lack presence
we don't ask questions
we compare
we try to impress
we obsess over things
with no significance

from here on out
take a pledge
to be intentional and genuine
in your interactions with other people
be deep
be true
be your higher self
just be you

the internet killed us all.

allow yourself the grace
to be vulnerable
we are imperfect
and require discomfort
to feel more comfortable

transformation.

love me like the stars

are you ready to spark a revolution
dare you dream
of a better future

democracy.

society
will marginalize me
and you
because
they know
we are too powerful
and that scares them

so
know your power
stand your ground
they will taunt you
do not falter
even if they lurk in the shadows
to try and drag you down

stand tall
stand proud
speak up
speak loud

they can't dim the light.

love me like the stars

i take the time
to embrace my past
forgiveness
is an important task
i can finally accept it
for what it is

struggle brought growth
sorrow brought a better tomorrow
the scars will remain
but i want
to live in joy
as opposed
to living with
a desolate soul
after all
we reap what we sow

you may say
you've endured so much sadness
so much pain
how does it just go away
well
i will tell you
what you must know

flowers can't grow in poisoned dirt
a caterpillar can't blossom into a butterfly
without first going through its cycles
the same can be thought about life
like all things
it's a process

you will be in pain
some moments will be unbearable
but time will heal
the cuts and the wounds
until one day
you don't feel the ache anymore

this can only happen
if you give yourself a chance
and permission
for it to disappear
you have to believe that
your circumstances
don't determine your path

it's perspective
it's a choice
i may have been hurt
but above all else
i choose to love

planting seeds of happiness.

before i moved to los angeles
i had just been laid off
i was surviving off of
unemployment benefits and welfare
i tried to conform
and settle once again
for a dead end job
where i would just exist
but i couldn't take it anymore
i was living in a box
i didn't want to just exist
i wanted to live

there was an urge in my soul
i could feel it in my gut
something told me *go*
and so
i packed up my bags
bought a one-way ticket to california
and left

i only had fifteen-hundred dollars
in my pocket
and i knew
i would struggle
but i also knew
that i was giving myself a chance
to live my dreams
and because i chose not to live in fear
my life has forever changed

and so the story goes.

i needed a reminder
that humanity isn't so bad
i needed confirmation
that my life
my ideas
my heart
were in the right place
that i could still create
and the world would care
i needed to know that
hope still existed
that real
living
breathing
people
cherished genuine connections
i needed to see that others believed
books are magic
that just the mere smell of written pages
brought us together
you restored that faith in me
because you were simply kind
i needed a spark
you gave me the spark
that birthed
my greatest work of art

the gift.

love me like the stars

and you
yes you
if you're wondering
what is left for you
the answer is everything

today may feel like
it is the end of all ends
but trust me
it's just the beginning
of your awakening

if you feel stuck
keep moving
take it step by step
inch by inch

if you're thinking of a new career
or contemplating building a new life
don't stop being a dreamer
don't stop putting up a fight

if you're feeling down
you will rise
if your heart feels like
it can't take it anymore
it will mend
slowly but surely
if your soul shakes with dismay
you will be at peace again

be gentle with yourself
be kind to yourself
be patient with yourself
rediscover yourself
confront yourself
love yourself
and emulate that out into the universe
because the energy you release
will find its way back to you tenfold

buy yourself flowers
lots of beautiful flowers
sit by the ocean
stand in the sun

pick up your pen
write out your anguish
let go of your pain
and the guilt ridden shame
don't live in the past
it can't change

but you hold the power to your present
you can and you will make a difference
look out for others
connect with others
i know it can be scary
but relationships
and even one conversation
will inspire you
they will feed your spirit
they will ignite your fire
and give you something
you never thought you needed
you have a future waiting to be created

everything will be ok
you
will
be
ok

rebirth.

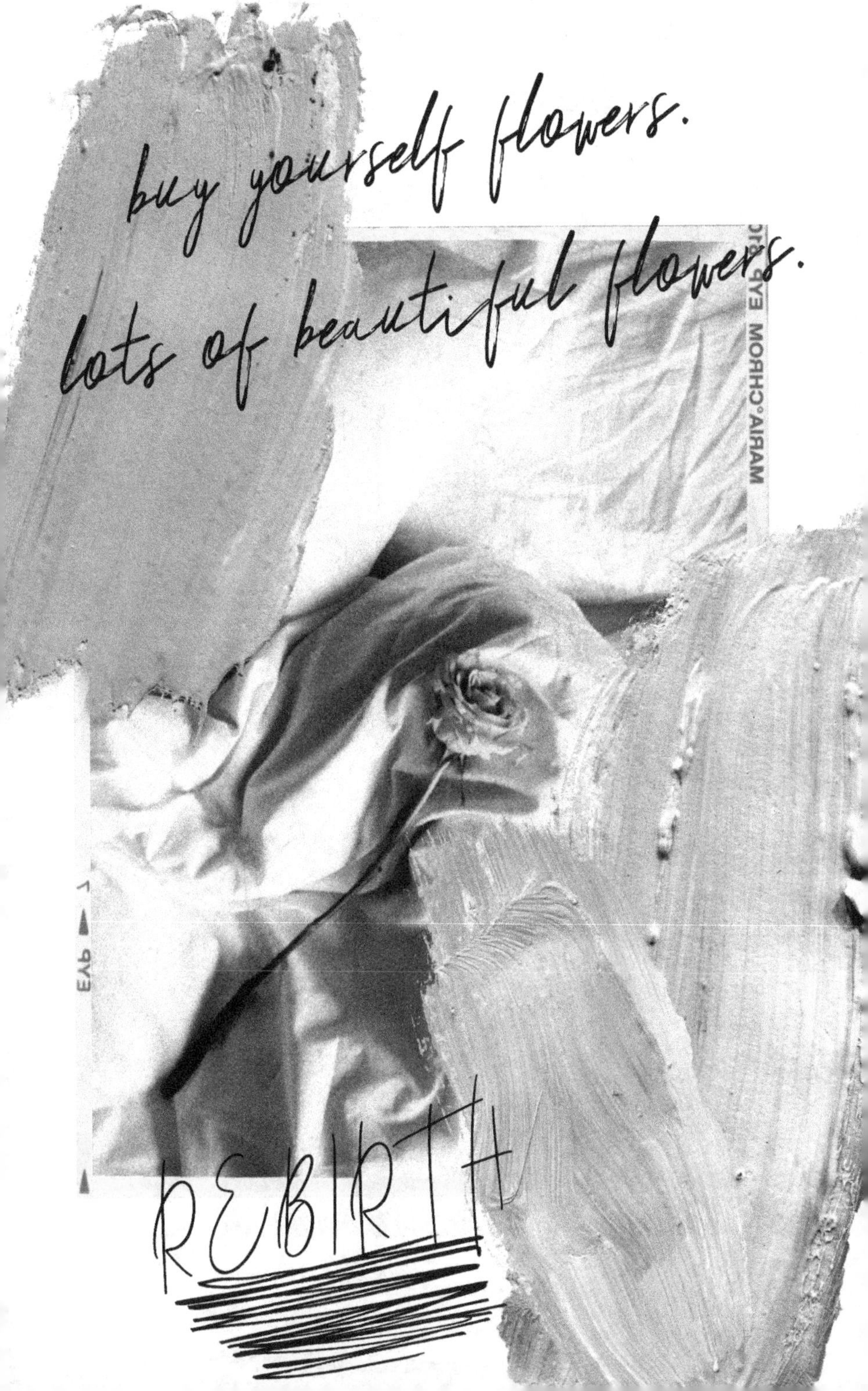
buy yourself flowers.
lots of beautiful flowers.
REBIRTH

THE GIFT

may you learn to love
the broken and most
unbeautiful pieces

you gave me the spark that birthed
my greatest work of art

about the ~~girl~~ author

creating art is nothing new to alesia, she discovered her passion for writing at the tender age of five and has used her love for it throughout life; you could always find her hiding behind a book, reading a new adventure every day. even at a young age, she knew that there was power in storytelling. as a creative director, influencer, photographer, activist and fashion designer - alesia is now able to share her heart with the world as an author. written in just 10 days, *love me like the stars* is her first compilation of poetry.

so i write these words knowing
you have no choice but to listen
do you hear me now?
or shall i speak louder?

about this book

love me like the stars is a collection of poetry and thoughts told through stories of lust, romance, heartache and salvation while navigating my journey as a woman of color. it's the love i've felt and lost. the heartache and the deep pain i've experienced. it's my road to recovery and healing. it's the salvation in my realizations. it's the culmination of my feelings. it's my frustration with our world's current state of being. every word is authentic to me. it's me literally pouring my heart out. it's me being the most vulnerable i have ever been. it's my way of connecting with you. to show you that you're not alone.

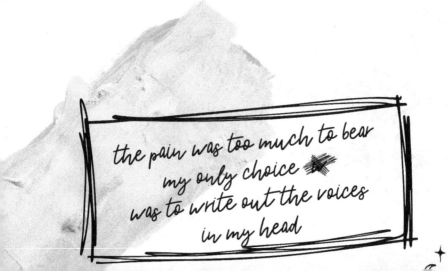

the pain was too much to bear
my only choice ✖
was to write out the voices
in my head

a monster's lullaby

they were hurting
i saw their open wounds
the monsters i saw
were the monsters in me too

i am their prisoner as they eat me slowly for dinner

they are drowning me in their pain

1-877-273-8255

the monsters call me
i try not to answer
but they hide under my bed
and in my closet

a monster's lullaby

this is my vulnerability.

you are the warmth
preposessing flowers
with an extravagant
love.

to stand up for what is right means
something. to speak up even if my tongue
feels heavy, means something.

dona nobis pacem

you inspire the most beautiful
sonnets that i could write / page after
page / the words come to life

the halo you wear shines
as bright as a thousand
stars in the night.
how beautiful it is
that we exist in the same
moment of time

allow yourself the grace
to be vulnerable
we are imperfect
and require discomfort
to feel more comfortable

sit by the ocean
stand in the sun

lust. romance. heartache.
salvation. lust. romance.
heartache. salvation. lust.
roma   t. on
lu
sa
he
rom   on
                         e.
salvation   n t. romance.
heartache. salvation. lust.
romance. heartache. salvation

if you're wondering what is left for
you: the answer is everything.
H a

WE TOUCH THE MOON. WE ARE ONE WITH THE STARS. SOARING THROUGH A GALAXY, MADE UP ENTIRELY OF OUR LUMINESCENT LOVE.

let me paint this lust into a work of art.

words by alesia carter

photography by alesia carter

page 250/253 - photography by virisa yong

page 254/middle photo - photography by sterling reed

page 256 - photography by virisa yong

page 257/middle photo - photography by virisa yong

page 258/259 - photography by virisa yong

creative direction, editing & art design by alesia carter

cover design by alesia carter

i am full of poetry
healing but still hurting
so i'll see you in
the next chapter of my story

CPSIA information can be obtained
at www.ICGtesting.com
Printed in the USA
LVHW080524030720
659501LV00004B/128